D1709498

Nancy Reagan

Jennifer Strand

abdopublishing.com

Published by Abdo Zoom™, PO Box 398166, Minneapolis, Minnesota 55439. Copyright © 2018 by Abdo Consulting Group, Inc. International copyrights reserved in all countries. No part of this book may be reproduced in any form without written permission from the publisher. Abdo Zoom™ is a trademark and logo of Abdo Consulting Group, Inc.

Printed in the United States of America, North Mankato, Minnesota
052017
092017

Cover Photo: Library of Congress
Interior Photos: Library of Congress, 1; Courtesy Ronald Reagan Library, 4, 5, 6, 7, 8, 9, 13, 14, 15, 17, 18, 19; AP Images, 10, 12; Ed Widdis/AP Images, 11; White House/AP Images, 16

Editor: Emily Temple
Series Designer: Madeline Berger
Art Direction: Dorothy Toth

Publisher's Cataloging-in-Publication Data
Names: Strand, Jennifer, author.
Title: Nancy Reagan / by Jennifer Strand.
Description: Minneapolis, MN : Abdo Zoom, 2018. | Series: First ladies |
    Includes bibliographical references and index.
Identifiers: LCCN 2017931129 | ISBN 9781532120183 (lib. bdg.) |
    ISBN 9781614797296 (ebook) | 9781614797852 (Read-to-me ebook)
Subjects: LCSH: Reagan, Nancy, 1964-2016--Juvenile literature. |Presidents
    spouses--United States--Biography--Juvenile literature.
Classification: DDC 973.927/092 [B]--dc23
LC record available at http://lccn.loc.gov/2017931129

Table of Contents

Introduction. 4

Early Life. 6

Leader. 10

First Lady 14

Legacy. 18

Quick Stats. 20

Key Dates .21

Glossary 22

Booklinks 23

Index 24

Introduction

Nancy Reagan was a First Lady of the United States.

The New Revolution IS "BEATING DRUG ABUSE"

PEP

Her husband was Ronald Reagan. She was known for working to stop drug use.

Early Life

Nancy was born on July 6, 1921.

Her mother was an actress.
Nancy wanted to be an actress, too.

She studied theater in college.

Then she acted in movies.
She used the name
Nancy Davis.

Leader

In 1952 Nancy married
Ronald Reagan.

He was an actor, too. Then he became **governor** of California.

As California's First Lady, Nancy worked on the Foster Grandparents program.

It connected young people with **elderly** mentors.

13

Nancy became the
US First Lady in 1981.

She **redecorated** the White House. She also hosted fancy parties.

Later Nancy made a program called "Just Say No."

It taught young people
to stay away from drugs.

Legacy

The Reagans left the White House in 1989.

Nancy continued working
to prevent drug use.
She died on March 6, 2016.

Nancy Reagan

Born: July 6, 1921

Birthplace: New York, New York

Husband: Ronald Reagan

Years Served: 1981–1989

Known For: Nancy Reagan was an actress and then a First Lady of the United States. She worked to prevent young people from using drugs.

Died: March 6, 2016

Key 📅 Dates

1921: Anne Frances Robbins is born on July 6. She is called Nancy.

1945: Nancy becomes an actress. She uses the name Nancy Davis.

1952: Nancy and Ronald Reagan marry on March 4.

1981-1989: Ronald Reagan is the 40th US president. Nancy Reagan is First Lady.

1981: The "Just Say No" program begins. Nancy started it to prevent drug use.

2016: Nancy dies on March 6.

Glossary

elderly - older, or later in life.

governor - a person who is the head of a state in the United States.

mentors - people who give help and advice to others.

program - a plan of action for achieving something, such as stopping drug use.

redecorate - to change the look of a house by painting walls, getting new furniture, and more.

Booklinks

For more information on
Nancy Reagan, please visit
abdobooklinks.com

Z**∘m** In on Biographies!

Learn even more with the Abdo Zoom
Biographies database. Check out
abdozoom.com for more information.

Index

actress, 7

born, 6

California, 11, 12

college, 8

died, 19

drug, 5, 17, 19

program, 12, 16

Reagan, Ronald, 5, 10, 18

White House, 15, 18

young people, 13, 17